Getting over It!

PRABADIP GHAI

"I dedicate this book to my late beloved & caring parents who left for their journey ahead to heaven, dedicate this book to my uncle & also to my little princess, my niece Sana (the fighter) whom we lost to the dreadful disease of cancer,"

"Words make an impact; they have the power to change lives,"

ILLNESS
FREEDOM
JOBS
LOANS
RELATIONS

About the book

Getting over it!

The book is the part of the book series money, jobs & business. The world is going through the worst ever economic & health crisis because of the pandemic. They forecast the future having limited earnings, economic slowdown & loss of jobs. It will make the life of individuals very much challenging as to run the show everyone needs fund. One has to ensure survival at both physical & economical level. The ever-changing business scenarios, technological advancements, very dynamic; consistent highs & lows of the financial market, unstable health and many more challenges in life may lead to a phase which is very painful emotionally, financially & professionally. This will make life very complex. Jobs are today at major risk of uncertainty. The long tenures are the days of past, office politics, changing dynamics, socio-economic influence & Loans deprive you of the luxury to be stable in a particular job or organization for long. Any day can be the last day in the organization, with or without explanations. I write the book intending to address the following questions which come into your mind while searching for a career or when you have to start afresh after the known or unknown challenges put a stop in your professional life. Can you correlate with the questions below?

Is there anything I can do?

Are there alternatives?

Any suggestions what should one do in this period of uncertainty?

Is doing a job the only solution?

Can we start something of our own?

Is there some way which can help me gauge my skills & competence?

Are there some tools to help me with knowing my potential strengths which I can make as an alternative career?

Where to get guidance from?

Can I start some earnings sitting at home?

How can my assets be used to reduce my liabilities?

I have seen many people who become advisors to people going through the period of pain in the life; without actually themselves having experienced the pain of what one may go through in the period of indecisiveness, confusion with jobs, selecting career & liabilities one must be carrying. When they have never experienced a sabbatical, they cannot understand what we have to go though? Then the question is who should you look up to for getting the right advice or guidance? I suggest a person who has come out tough through the process, struggled & survived against odds will be the right one to guide. The author himself has witnessed sabbatical 3 times in his professional career. He has been a people's manager, easily approachable; lending his ears & helping people with timely guidance & advice from his life experiences. This book summarizes all experiences of 10 years of struggle with employment & a low profile. The author talks about options, Do's & Don'ts in the period of sabbatical. The input is through various interviews & experiences of people along with his own. This book talks about experiences of how people started from scratch again in life. The purpose of the book is to help people find options, solutions and alternatives before & during the period of sabbatical. It may be mutual or forced exit from the job. There can be any reason for the exit, but the challenges related to it are almost the same & inevitable. Everyone needs funds to run their life. Whatever savings one may have, gets exhausted because of lack of inflow. We have to be emotionally mature & have to execute everything professionally. This will help us come out strong, smiling, shining & successful. This is the right way through the metamorphosis.

Roads never end in professional life; they just take some unexpected turns.

-Prabadip Ghai

Sometimes because of economic situations, practical issues & for change in business around the globe, things may not work as your dream plan. It is ok! Life does not come to a dead-end with it. It is just a turn, not a dead end. Circumstances may call you to come up with something extraordinary. So just chill, relax & redesign your strategy of life. You may find it difficult as many of us get badly attached with companies, associates, colleagues & bosses. I have a sincere advice; never get attached to brands & companies. Make your professional goals & objectives clear. Target is to earn for yourself & your family. It may be an X company or Y company, it does not make a difference until you are getting paid what you deserve. The goal is to have those currency notes in your wallet in good numbers. It is essential to sustain your status quo. Please understand just one-stop does not end your professional journey

Who should read the book?

The target readers are the ones who are planning to start their career & require guidance on how and what to choose. This book covers a good number of do's & don'ts to follow while applying for a job. Book also provides practical solutions to choose for an alternative career or to start a professional life or start a journey as an entrepreneur. Intent is to help people who may be going through the painful & emotional period of sabbatical. Book also has a touch of psychological & spiritual solutions for the challenging periods in life. Book has a purpose to provide a complete package of guidance which may be required as per the writer who himself has faced & experienced the tough periods in professional life & started from ground zero financially. There are practical advices & solutions in the book. Author has explained these in very simple language that people having a little knowledge of the English language can easily understand & the aim is to reach global readers & touch over a million lives.

The author humbly requests to readers who go through the book & understand the worth, kindly suggests it to as many readers as they can; we never know the book may help someone in need.

INDEX

PLAN B: The alternative earning mode

The best way to revive is to pause & rethink your life.

-Unknown

Acknowledgement

I would like to acknowledge many people in my life. I would offer my gratitude to the group of individuals who have helped me emotionally & monetarily in my life to rise again. These are the ones who mentored me to learn lessons of my life. I offer my gratitude to my parents (My Father Lt. Shri Darshan Kumar Ghai & my mother Smt. Sharda Rani Ghai) who are in light & had put in all the efforts possible that made me who I am today. Without a consistent push from my parents made, it would not have been possible. I would like to thank all those people in life, those who came as a lesson for life in my professional & personal life. These are the people who helped me the experience & strengthen through professional challenges they brought with them. I firmly believe everything happens for a reason & would like to thank my family specially my better half Diptie who has always been taking care of me and giving me full independence to pursue my dreams by taking care of everything back in the family. I would also like to acknowledge the most important person, my spiritual guide, my mentor in my inner journey, Ms. Manmeet Kumar helped me strengthen in my spiritual journey and also made me understand life as a soul & my soul journey. She helped me understand the soul contracts, life lessons & that everything is caused by vibrations which we send to the universe & also helped me know & develop the "Attitude of Gratitude."

How can I leave my kids alone? My son Prieyansh always supports me in whatever I do & my daughter Rupahnshni being the biggest critic, always inspiring me to think different & think big. The author will also like to thank extended family on FB, my cousin, brother & guide Mr. Vikas Mehra, my younger brothers Sandeep Sir & Mandeep and my childhood friends who never failed to inspire me to do much better. My gratitude to my brother-in-law Ashish & my best pal Ritu, who has been standing beside me through my thick & thin of life; would finally end this acknowledging with gratitude to the universe to let me experience the challenges which enabled me to write this book which,I am sure will help many people who during & post-pandemic might face challenges of a break in career. I offer my special thanks to my friend, Sahdeep Sharma, for making value additions which have made this book more attractive with his artwork & suggested improvements.

(I have used some images from the internet, study from various sites & interviewed many people going through or went through sabbatical)

Failure is the opportunity to begin again, more intelligently.

-Henry Ford

COVID '19
QUARANTINE
Sandeep '20

Getting into Job again

"Revisiting the Plan A,"

If it is important for you, you will find out a way if not, you will have a million excuses

"By Unknown

Keep your morale high as ups & downs are part of professional life:-

The biggest & most important thing is not to lose cool & panic. The calm mind can breed hundred & thousands of solutions, which is the most important thing in the period of uncertainty. There may be a thousand thoughts which will feed your mind with negativity but keep on reminding yourself that after so many years of life it is you who has been earning using your learning's, skill set & experience. The one incident or an event cannot undermine your potential. You are much above the defined failures which are just part of professional life. Ups & downs will be there in professional life. Problem is just an unusual complex situation which can be outnumbered with solutions by applying your skill & solution-oriented mind-set. "Law of attraction" suggests, "What you will emphasize upon will magnify so **magnify what you need & not what you fear**". There is a famous saying in India "Man ke hare harhai man ke jete jeet"

"If you lose hope, you lose the war" Which means you do not lose until you lose the hope to win. You must only focus on win & restructure your thoughts with the will &

manifest to rise again. There will be many people with the number of questions analyzing, judging and even mocking you on your failures. Just let them do their work as more you explain or respond to, it will make you lose your focus. Just let them be the mock spectator.

Patience & perseverance:-

Life is unpredictable. When challenged by situations you never planned for, the best strategy is to have patience & perseverance. In case you get stressed out with overthinking you will panic & the mind stops working. You will run around directionless, not getting anywhere & killing your chances to stabilize. I advise it to keep calm & maintain cool, take a silent gap, devise your strategy, go through your contact & email list of people you know personally & professionally. Check if some one has been through the situation & has made it back up to the position. Perseverance & faith work miracles. We should use them to optimize our self in the situation; which is unique to us.

It's my humble suggestion to each & every person who is reading the book & is also going through a sabbatical (Job loss).

"There are no dead ends in professional life, there are just unexpected turns "-Prabadip Ghai

Turn a deaf ear to negativity: -

Accept no one's definition of your life; define it yourself.

-Harvey Fierstein

You may meet many people in your professional & business life who are not contributing any way in your life. These words & negativity, if you grab, will create the biggest barrier in your life. Do not just accept anything which is being given to you as advice or caution. The belief system of other people is not your belief; they may be on a self consolation drive because they could not achieve in their life. One failure does not define you; it is how you rebound & rise after many failures makes you who you are. A piece of very important advice is to turn a deaf ear to negativity and focus on what you want to achieve.

Time Management: -

The most important part of life is time. It comes with an equal opportunity for everyone irrespective of age, region, caste, creed & profession. Everyone has an equal opportunity to use time. There is a misnomer that we can manage time rather than we have to align ourselves & prioritize things which are important & essential. Focus on what is important & urgent rather than creating an atmosphere of self-pity. "What should I do now? How should I do?" We have to know & practice a sense of urgency. Whenever we are in a situation, we need to get our self in action & get going. More we delay the more we lose. The opportunities to earn are always there, but they are time bound. Plan your day & plan your activity during the day as per priority. **Being occupied does not mean that you are productive**. You may be occupied with things which are not even worth, and you postpone things essential in your life. This way you add distance to your success. The most important aspect of being successful is how you use your time. Invest it wisely on self-development & do not run after how to do it rather learn from people who have already done it successfully. This will help you save the time to reinvent the wheel.

Make a list of consultants with numbers & email ids:-

The most important & the first activity is to make a list of professional consultants. This activity would help you get in touch with experienced & thorough professionals in the field. This list will be a step forward to your effort to stabilize & stand back on your feet again. The best way to be back in the market is to use professional expertise to find the right job for you. The professionals will be the right ones to find a suitable opportunity as they have a network in the industry through their networking skills & years of experience in recruitment. They are well trained in their professional work, more suitable & well equipped to search the right break for you. Make calls to the consultants & discuss your state to make them understand your situation, get their email id's & forward your

Resume/CV after getting the Resume/CV in the right format, Preferably professionally made.

Update your CV:-

As suggested in the previous paragraph the foremost thing is to get your CV updated. There are various sites which provide facilities of a professional CV making at nominal charges.

I always suggest to have a professional CV, as this is your first impression you create in the recruiter's mind. There are following things which you should keep in mind while making your CV/or getting it made. Ensure the following things.

CV should be limited to 2 to 3 pages only.

Highlight professional achievements.

Do not make details of everything you do.

Highlight your key skills.

Do not forget to put at least two professional references in your CV.

Ensure proper formatting.

Always forward your CV in PDF form, which avoids distortion & formatting issues.

Do not do bulk forwarding of your CV as it will go in the spam folders.

Please ensure to mention your LinkedIn profile link on your CV.

Mention the time when you should be contacted.

Before circulating, the CV please ensure proof reading for any clerical mistakes in your CV, which will create a negative impression in the recruiter's mind.

Your CV is your ambassador, Ensure all measures to make it professional.

Connect & make a call to professional consultants to help find you a Job:-

When you have completed updating your CV & your CV is well-drafted, now is the time to circulate it to professional consultants in Job market. Collect data of the mobile numbers of consultants call them & discuss the job openings related to your area of expertise. After the discussion, note down the email id of the placement consultant to forward your CV/Resume.

Avoid sending emails randomly without calling & discussing as this will not get the right attention that your CV needs. Please ensure following points discussed with the consultant you are calling

Area of expertise.

Special skill set.

Share about your preferred profile & expected CTC.

Express your willingness to shift to another location.

Please specify at least three preferred locations where you can move.

These things will help consultant have clarity on your options which he can zero down to the right job. This will help them find the right fit & make the recruitment process easier.

Connect with your mentors & professional references in the Industry:-

Every professional in Industry grows under the guidance of professional mentors & bosses. They train the individuals & they understand well the professional in them. It would be the right thing to make calls to your professional mentors & to update them you are available in the job market for your next career move. It is always a better thing to work with earlier bosses as you already share a bond & establishing yourself with them will not take much of a time. This will save you the waiting time & avoid lengthy interview processes, moreover boosting your morale, which is an added advantage. Please understand every individual in the job has to follow some set rules of organization & procedures which may limit their authority & power to take you directly on board. Please do not overemphasize or push your case too far. This may leave a sour taste if things do not materialize. The senior may also feel low for not being able to put you through. It is better to ensure not pressing beyond certain limits. This does not limit your need to follow-up, but limit the frequency of follow-up.

Search Jobs through LinkedIn:-

LinkedIn is a professional site with lot many options. Have a professional profile made on LinkedIn site. This site also allows you to connect with your colleagues, professional references, consultants & moreover this site brings in the best of Jobs in industry. The LinkedIn site has options for seeking professional recommendations from people who have worked with you, your bosses, Peers & your team mates. This is like a 360-degree appraisal where people write about you & their experiences working with you & also write their professional recommendations. This may be the right tool to use for your next move in the career. They make your profile, including with your key skills sets. Your professional achievements & your recommendations on skill sets by professionals in the network are a great boon. The LinkedIn site provides options for paid services which are a premium service which helps you to get Job offers & apply through LinkedIn premium. There are options to block particular industry & people to see your profile like on Face book.

Identify your key skills & identify your gaps:-

Make a list of your skill set. This will help you know your key strengths & help identify gaps which you need to work upon. It requires these gaps to be filled and to achieve a better career. It is an excellent thing to know about the gaps, aka weaknesses. This will help you to find whom to look at for guidance, identify your need for training or professional courses which will help you fill these identified gaps. You better invest in increasing your skill sets through various professional courses, training & seminars, which will help you to have a refresher. These trainings may also help you upgrade your information about the latest trends in the industry from the speakers who are masters in their field. It is always good to know your key strengths as the interviewer may ask you about your key strengths & also about your weaknesses. When you have a ready list prepared.It will be a simple job to explain it to the interviewer with full confidence.

Make a professional write up of your experiences as a case study & update your knowledge:-

It would be a good reference & a reckoner when you write your professional experience as a case study. This will become a ready reckoner for you to prepare well for your interviews. This will help you avoid missing any achievement of your professional life. It will also help you explain during the interview how you carried out tasks/projects in your professional life. The interviewers are more interested in such case studies on how you handled, tackled or resolved any issues/hindrances in your professional life.

Watch YouTube videos on trainings related to your field.

Subscribe for Scribd and other sites for professional presentations on topics related to your area of expertise.

Google search for topics of your interest.

These activities will keep you busy, productive, will enhance & refresh your knowledge. Learning will also boost your morale & will avoid any depression or feeling of a failure coming into your mind. Make notes of your learning's in your diary, good to use for future reference & revision of what were the points you learned. It will be great to make a "watch later" list on YouTube of videos which you liked. This will save you the effort to search these videos again. Also, download Google pages for future references for learning. Download e-books related to life, motivation & public speaking. This will help you keep yourself motivated. Public speaking is the most important skill in any professional sphere, along with the presentation skills. If you can get the right coach to help you work upon these key skill sets, it would be a great boon to your career. It will help you crack interviews through the use of right postures, body language, use of right words & professional, confident explanation of your experience & expertize. Interviews are sessions of selling your professional expertise in 30 minutes to 45 minutes & to create the right impression. Always remember there is no second chance to make a first impression.

Forward your CV on job portals:-

Whenever you are using Job portal to apply for jobs, please ensure that you use the email id of the recruiter to email directly. Use the email id written along with the contact number. There are over 1000 applicants for a particular job which may match their profile.Applying directly through the portals may not get the attention of recruiter as there will be large number of applicants. To make your CV seen as a priority applicant, follow the following points

Use direct email ids of the recruiter to send your CV.

Make an impressive cover letter.

Keep on updating your profile on Job portals.

Make your profile on multiple job portals Like Naukri.com, Times jobs, Shine, Monster, Job tokri & LinkedIn.

Forward your resume/ CV to professional consultants Randstad, JAC, Team Pasona, Michael page, Stanton chase, Executive access, Adecco, Unison Consultants, Symbiosis etc to mention are a few professional ones.

Apply for the job, matching most appropriately with your profile.

Keep updating your profile every week; it will display your CV among the first few.

Get your CV professionally made as it is your first impression.

Do not bulk forward your resume to save time as your CV will land up in spam folder,

Keep on checking updates & job recommendations.

Things necessary after making applications on portals:-

There are options to check your application status where you can know whether your application has been viewed by the recruiter

Following things is a must in your things-to-Do list:-

Keep your mobile number & email id updated on Job portals.

Always mention your most used /checked email id.

Pick all the calls, you never know which call is from the prospective employer, if you miss one please ensure to call back, it is professional ettiquette to call back.

Check your emails frequently not to miss any job offer.

Respond to all relevant emails from consultants.

Check the feedback of the company you are applying from sites like Glass door to know the culture of the company.

Always check the salary range if mentioned as you avoid applying for low-paid jobs.

We should also check location of the job to ensure you apply for most relevant jobs.

Go through the Job description & required experience.

Organizations usually give their preference to people from similar industry so you also check for the same before applying to avoid not getting shortlisted & wasting one opportunity.

Do not apply through multiple consultants for the same job.

Most important points to follow in the no job period:-

Ensure to have a medical policy for the entire family intact.

Reduce your financial liabilities like loans, etc.

Invest wisely.

Do not borrow heavy amounts out of fear.

Pay your EMI's on time.

Do not withdraw from PF's & other social security funds.

Keep yourself fit, set an exercise schedule.

Listen to favorite music to upkeep your mood.

Meditate & listen to chants.

Travel & socialize whenever it is necessary.

Meet people who have something constructive to say.

Attend professional seminars, online webinars.

Read excellent books.

Keep yourself busy. Sitting & doing nothing will not help you.

Do not panic, always stay organized & structured in your approach:-

This period of sabbatical (forced/optional) is very challenging. In desperation, we make many mistakes which have to be avoided at any cost. Most of the people make silly mistakes. This period requires you to be calm & structured in your approach. The challenge is enormous as you have to understand the losing job is part of professional life. Most of the time, it is the business scenario which causes retrenchment. A few times some documentary issues, audit failures, failures in compliances, office politics & sometimes you are a scape goat for bigger organizational politics. It is ok as it is part of the professional life. The only thing you need to keep in mind is that it is not the end of the world & the company you were working for is not the last organization. Avoid making the following mistakes.

Do not write tag lines on job portals & LinkedIn "Desperately looking for a job" You have to be professional in the words you use & write on any social media. Companies prefer to hire people who have a powerful will & know how to tackle situations. They do not look for the ones who are seeking sympathy, cooking stories, blaming people. It is always a wonderful thing to work upon moving ahead rather than focusing on what went wrong. If not, then you will lose a crucial period where you can lose many opportunities in the picture. Focus on the moment, if you continue in the job to find the right job & the entire focus must be on finding the right one.

Do not go for consultants charging for registrations of your resume/CV:-

Many pseudo consultants are sitting in the job market especially in Asean countries who will charge a few dollars$ in the name of registration of your CV in their data bank. The professional consultants will never charge from the job seeker, rather they bill to the organization seeking the employees.

Do not get trapped in fake job calls & offers:-

As you post on job portals & start applying for a job regularly, fake job offers will start pouring in. There will be many calls on your phone confirming jobs in hand with them & will ask you to pay some decent amount for registration for the job. These people are fake, they can even hack your accounts used for making payments. No website offering jobs offer these kinds of services when you are desperate for a job. They can easily lure you in their trap with fake job commitments & even fake LOI's of the job from the company. You will realize it once they trap you & then they do not lift the calls & numbers are not traceable. Countries like Pakistan, Srilanka, India & other Asian countries. India being an enormous country & limited resources in cyber crime resolution, it is nearly impossible to track these people & you lose your money in a crucial period when you need to conserve it to the maximum.

Do not explain to everyone:-

When you are in a low period in your professional life, People in your circle may be interested in knowing your story. I would suggest not everyone has a genuine concern for you; many of them will talk behind your back & try to belittle you. You may become a topic of discussion in your professional circle. People will treat you with indifference. If you explain to everyone & brief your story more gossips will go around & reference checks get a negative impact. People think you must be wrong or must have done something wrong. Some people out of professional jealousy, some just for fun and some just as a habit will talk behind you, more the gossips going around, more damage & more it will tarnish your professional image. I have heard people saying without knowing details, "I don't know, but I heard XYZ about him /her". They take this straight as opinion & any iota of doubt reduces your chances of selection in a recent job opportunity by 90% until there is someone in the system that knows you in erson & has an original opinion. The best part is stopping explaining to any Tom, Dick & Harry as they won't add value but may cause serious damage to your professional image. Whether you like it or not, there are a team of people who are gossip mongers, they spread rumors around you just to check people's reaction & then let this information spread loss in the professional market. It is the biggest threat to your professional life. Either you are in the strongest position in your professional life, people who cannot succeed by their potential, love to see successful people fall.

Do not just call anyone to seek help for a job:-

Not everyone is your friend & not everyone is your enemy in professional life. People react based on your position. I advise not to seek help from just anyone. Not everyone has potential & intention to help. Do not just run around to everyone seeking help for the job, I suggest a "BIG NO". I would advise you to seek help only from professional recruitment consultants & from your professional mentors & guides.

Do not withdraw all your Social Security funds, PF, other savings & retirals:-

In the situation of financial stress, it is a common tendency that you withdraw PF and other savings immediately. I advise that you should not withdraw the finances immediately. At least wait for a month or two. In case you have an option to use the money you withdraw to pay off debts, loans to reduce financial stress you can use the same. Limit spends to just things which are necessities. Limit your spending as this is a moment where more you conserve your resources, more you are in a better situation.

I strictly advise that we should keep social security funds for the old age or tough rainy days.

Resume circulation services are of little or no use:-

I did not find services like resume blaster; resume zapper etc of any benefit. My suggestion would be to avoid spending on such services. Still, you can go ahead with your free will to use such services.

Do not just apply for any job:-

There is a limit to the daily job application & monthly job application. It is better to be very selective in applying for jobs. Please apply for most relevant jobs only to use the provided allocated quota of application wisely.

Few points for interview:-

Never fake about your job. It is not bad to have a break period in professional life.

Do not speak ill about your past organizations or previous bosses, it harms your credibility.

Avoid creating a sob story for seeking sympathy as told earlier in explaining points. Organizations look for winners & solution finders, not the ones who find excuses.

Prepare well for your reason of break, it would help raise fewest concerns on your exit from the previous organization during the interview.

Do not say something which is not relevant or fake. This will be a disaster. Times are challenging. There is no second thought to what all can bring in a new situation which may bring you to ground zero, where you need to rethink of your life. Create the life of your dreams out of your zone of command & comfort. Many times life will throw you into a situation where your traditional employment cannot continue for whatever reason.

Now the list of questions that will come into your mind are:-

What should I do now?

I don't know where to start?

What are the options for me?

Where to look for solutions?

Who can help me?

Can I use my current skill set & experience to do something of my own?

To do business I will need funds, how & from where can I get funds to start?

Is there anything which I can start on my own without investments?

In how much time can I reach to a level, where I do not have to worry about my earnings?

Will I be able to do things on my own?

What are the websites for alternative jobs?

How to find Links where I can get information to do my work?

Can I do something from my home?

How would I know what are the work I can do?

What are the methods & tools for self-evaluation?

How to use these tools?

How to identify the best out of it?

What is the list of options I have?

Is job only the solution with my kind of education?

Procrastination kills my confidence, what should I do?

Keeping yourself strong:-

When one is not in the job, there are a lot of questions, unrest, instability, social pressures, family pressures & a lot of turbulence in the mind? It calls for a lot of calmness & capacity to ignore external pressures. The biggest need of the hour is to calm down, stabilize your mental & emotional state through the turmoil. This will not only ensure your recovery but also prevent mental, physical & emotional hazards.

Use the following for your mental, emotional & physical health:-

Start exercise routine: -

This period is a golden period in disguise. Make the best use of it. Because of occupancy & too much workload, we forget to upkeep our physical health. This period allows you to focus on physical health & to work upon it. I must remind you at this point only a healthy body can perform under pressure, both mentally & physically. The sabbatical period allows you to work upon yourself to be fit for recent challenges life is throwing at you. A well equipped, well trained, fully motivated & a mentally prepared warrior who is ready to sacrifice everything for the purpose will to win the war. Be the one! Exercise will not only add to your physical health, but will also improve your persona. As a professional, you require to carry yourself well. It will help to make a positive impact with the right body structure, being physically fit and a mix of right attitude & right body language. When you are physically & mentally fit you exhibit non-verbal confidence which impresses everyone.

Meditate: -

As there will be physical pressures & challenges and there will be mental stress. The best way to cope with these pressures is to meditate. Meditation has nothing to do with being religious & chanting mantras etc. Mediation is the inward journey. Focus more on unifying your thoughts and coming to a no-thought state. In meditation, the focus is on monitoring your breath & practice breathing with a special pattern/technique. This will increase your concentration & make you strong emotionally & mentally. Meditation is the most powerful tool to increase your mental potential and makes you emotionally stable. This period will require you to be positive, affirmative, healthy & stable; we can define it as to be in a state where you can make right decisions, stop reacting & be structured in your approach. There are a lot of guided meditations available online on YouTube. You can choose any of them & meditate, being in self-imposed isolation with no disturbances, with the help you get the best results with meditation. During meditation & rejuvenation, one must adapt to drinking more water.

Ensure to have a medical checkup: -

In this period, implement every check measure to ensure you are healthy & strong. I advise it to have a complete health check-up. Prevention is always better than cure. Go for a medical check-up & have a medical policy in place for the entire family. I have witnessed many people in this period facing medical emergency & hospitalization. A cow attacked one of my friends in the period of forced sabbatical & had to be hospitalized for almost a week. He was lucky to have a medical policy in place. The cost of hospitalization was almost around one-tenth of a million. If he had no medical, it could have been a sizeable hole in the pocket in the critical period. It is always better to have an on-cost of a medical policy of your own if you think it is an on cost. Medical policy is your financial nectar in case of emergency. The medical checkup may highlight some parameters where you need to focus to remain fit for extra challenges of life. I would like to re-emphasize & reiterate, please ensure a thorough medical checkup & medical policy in place for your family, including your parents.

Deep breath: -

Breathing is an excellent way to calm your thoughts & improve your oxygen intake. Deep breathing is always good but in fresh air & clean environment. On a lighter note, rather involve entire family members into this routine as they also require developing the patience to bear a person at home who will now be present most of the time, noticing, commenting & trying to correct everything interfering in their personal space & routine. Just to caution you, you may find it being responsible, but they may not welcome you at all.

Walk a few miles: -

 Walking will help you on the health front and give you time with yourself to introspect. Walking with light music through ear leads will be most comforting & will give you time to test yourself; create strategies, think way forward. This will help you improve your cardiac health which in most has an issue because of professional concerns & occupancies, developing unwelcomed stress in body & straining your heart the most. The heart is the engine of your life & it needs to be healthy & running all the time. The heart needs fresh air, less stress, healthy & clean (unblocked) nerves to function to its best. I am not a doctor, but the experiences in life have made me to learn on being healthy. I being diabetic myself; I am more prone to health hazards related to kidney & heart. Walking is the best of exercise to ensure a healthy body by burning fat, adding to oxygen intake, removes toxins. This will also help you with healthier & strong bones; reduce blood pressure, enhance your lung capacity & take control of sugar levels in the body. Being healthy, mentally fit, emotionally strong & experienced professional in your field makes you an ideal candidate organizations are looking for.

Develop a hobby: -

Hobbies are things which you love to do; it motivates you, boosts your morale, makes you take part & above all keeps you busy out of the emotional & mental shit you may experience in your period of low in life. You can work on things you love to do since your childhood or you wanted to do but could never do for any reason. Develop that strength in yourself to relive your dreams of childhood. Work on those hobbies, be strong, be innovative, be at your best with the things you love to do. You may also find an opportunity in your hobby which will get the best performance out of you as you will do what you love to do. Identify your hobbies, list them down, See which hobby connects you to the most & gives you Goosebumps. Work on it and establish a bond with the hobbies again. Identify that can this be a medium which may help you earn some monetary benefits. If yes, plan a strategy around it and start executing it to be a bread earning activity may be a secondary source of income or the primary one if it can get you the right amount needed to run your daily needs with ease.

Write a page daily at night: -

It's a traditionally known way & very much practiced technique. All successful people use it to review the output & critical learning points to remember from the day. This will help you recollect the activities of the day & also help you know the gaps. We can use it for future references. Diary writing will also help as a record of your experience & learning which may a reference & a guide to people going through similar situations. Your writing may be a tool for someone who can learn from your experiences on mistakes & the actions for problem-solving. More than anyone else it is an evaluation technique for you to gauge your performance & the ways to correct yourself for the future. This will help you grow & will help you express your feelings which if vented out, easing your emotional state of mind. Expressing yourself by any mean or medium is the best way to balance yourself & distant yourself from negativity. As expressed earlier a healthy state of emotional & mental health along with physical wellbeing is very important in phases of lives; with potent challenges which put you in a do or die situation. Be healthy & stay fit for your well being.

<u>Read books & watch videos associated with learning:</u> - Upgrading oneself is very important, not only during the phase of challenging times but also during the period of regularity in employment, to rise in a professional ladder. Reading books is the best way to keep you abreast with the market. Read at least two books in a month. If you are the one who is fond of reading nothing can stop you. Books not only upgrade your knowledge but also keep you confident & motivated. In today's word, with most of the work on laptops & smart phones, online read e-books through kindle subscription. If you are a no book person, then you have the option of learning through videos. The world is going digital & you have access to the internet at even the remotest places in the country you live in. This helps you have access to any learning video online at any hour of the day at your convenience. The subscription is free with advertisements in between & with no ads with the subscription. Both are ok as the breaks in between the ads are of few seconds to 2 minutes. Based on your history of browsing videos, YouTube will automatically suggest videos for you to learn to reduce your time to search for relevant videos. Make a practice to always keep a note pad for yourself to note-down critical points for your reference & some important learning is which you can use to refresh your learning's at a later time.

Practice mudras for overall well being: -

There is a lot of literature on mediation & spirituality on line. Mudras are also an important part of a body expression of energies to balance, enrich & release of energies. There are a lot of sites, from sadguru to various other leaders in spirituality & meditation. These mudras help improve your physical being. They help remove the low charges from the body & balance your energies

"The mind & body are not separate entities. The gross form of the mind is the body & the subtle form of the body is the mind. The practice of asana integrates & harmonizes the two. Both the body & the mind harbor tensions or knots. Every mental knot has a corresponding physical, muscular knot & vice versa. Asana aims to release these knots. Asana help to ease mental tensions by dealing with them on the physical level, acting somato psychically, through the body to the mind."

– **Swami SatyanandaSaraswati,**

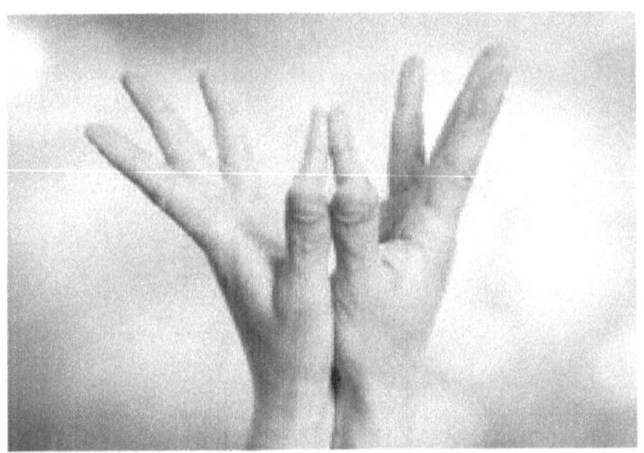

Mudras

1. Gyan Mudras for Healing Power:
   Benefits Towards Health:
   - This gyan hand mudra helps to relax your mind and improve
   - The ability to concentrate better. It keeps brain power sharp and smart.
   - It can cure insomnia (inability to sleep)

Regular practice can keep you stress relief and depression.

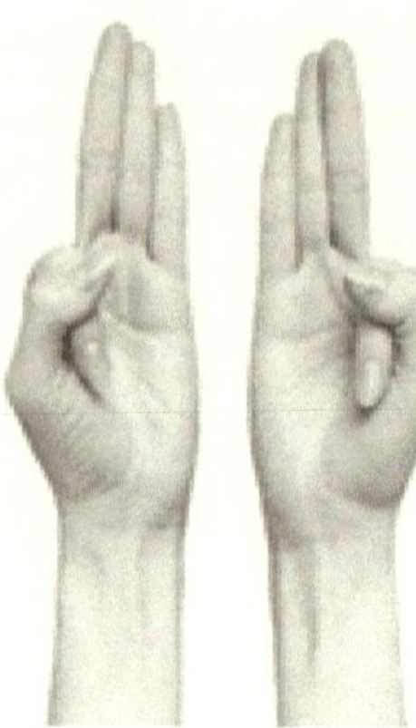

Benefits: Vayu Mudra

- This yoga mudras eliminates excessive gas from your body
- It can gives relief in problems associated with the air element such as: Flatulence, constipation, cervical spondylitis, arthritis etc

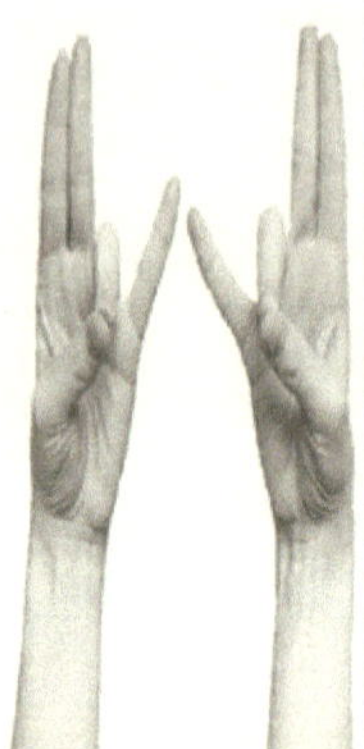

Prithvi Mudra Benefits:

1. This mudra gesture balances the element Earth in your body.
2. It improves body weight, blood circulation, digestive power and vitamin deficiency associated problems.

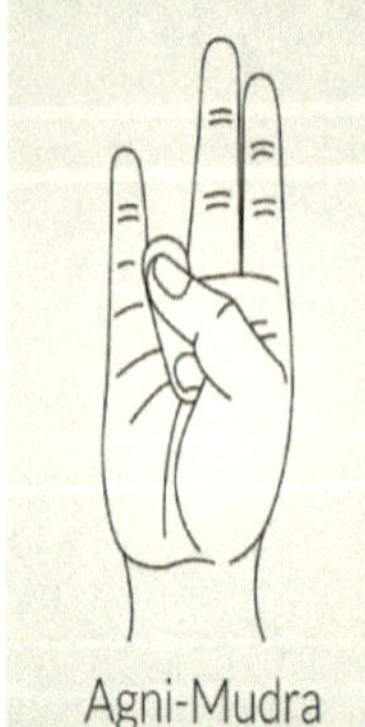

Agni-Mudra

Benefits: Agni Mudra

1. It helps to reduce the levels of Cholesterol in the
2. Body, reduces fats,
3. Improves metabolism
4. Boost the Immune System.

And many more which will help you find a cure & mental peace

<u>Spend some time with nature:</u> -We all are the part of the universe & nature. The best part of being with nature is relaxing & detoxifying. Whenever you are in stress & distress, try your hands at gardening.It will relieve you & comfort you. Mother earth absorbs all negative charges. It relaxes your brain and comforts your body. If you recollect, in our childhood we used to play in mud, water, rain & we rarely fell ill. We were amongst the happiest generation who enjoyed the transition from 20th century to 21st century. We played games in open grounds, grass & water. This would help us be stress free as compared to today's generation. Yes, we have developed but our touch with nature has reduced drastically; we have contributed only negatively to the environment & not worked much on the things that would benefit the environment. Sit among the trees & shrubs. Watch flying birds, listen to flowing water or go for sun gazing early morning. All elements of nature relax you & help you get rid of toxicity.

<u>Watch fishes in an aquarium</u>: -Since childhood fishes have always attracted us. Many of the childhood poems have been around fishes. We loved to know & act like fishes. Have you ever tried watching fishes flowing in an aquarium? It is being tested, tried & proved scientifically that watching fishes flowing calms down anxiety & reduce stress. You can spend hours watching fishes without getting tired & you remove toxins from your brain & body.

<u>Listen to fast music to elevate your mood:</u>-Music is the best tool to change your mind, state & mood. It depends on the music which you are listening to. Whenever you are in a low mood to listen to fast music, this will change the pace of your thoughts. It will elevate your mood, make you happy & raise your vibrations. Music is the best treatment for your mind & soul. Vibrations & different frequencies of music impact the body of the person listening & exposed to it. Some music frequencies are also used to meditate; it releases all negative accumulation of thoughts & has an immediate impact on your mind. The music can divert you from any mood to an original mind state altogether. Music is an effective healing tool, science also proves that music helps release favorable & relaxing chemicals in the body good for the human mind & physical body. Music helps improve self-expression. We also use music therapy as a treatment for elderly people suffering from Alzheimer's disease. It improves communication, social, sensory, cognitive, physical & emotional skills. Music is a free therapy.

Draw: -

Drawing is also a medium of expression. It improves creativity & concentration. We also use the colors which are used in drawing in the alternative treatment of depression. The drawing needs imagination, which involves you & helps your mind to concentrate; this will not only keep you busy but also avoid many distractions, social, mental & professional. Drawing is a representation of one's mind & personality. You can speak your mind with your drawings. So use your imagination, create& draw your mind on the canvas. You will grow with peace of mind, stability & patience, which is most needed when you are going through a phase of transition & making efforts to rise again after the fall. It requires a lot of courage to rise after a professional disaster with a lot of questioning eyes, a hell lot of gossips, character assassination happening around you which can drain anyone emotionally and socially. It may take years for you to come out & face in open.

Write blogs: -

When you work with the word, write blogs. Today several people have set the social stage on fire by using blogs as a medium of expression. The people with very sound control on vocabulary and know how to use words to create magic. The keywords will bring many people on their blogs & not only make one famous with write-ups but also can be a source of earning through traffic on their blog by putting Google ads & other similar methods paying against several visits on your blogs. These things will increase your social presence, boost your morale & will increase your chances to network with the right people. There are many options for writing blogs, one of the blog is WordPress.com. You can create a free profile and you can express yourself in words. Use your social network & connections to increase your views.

Limit general socialization, focus only on networking & learning: -

I strictly advise to limit socialization as a lot of questions will kill your mental peace. You can also have issues of complex comparing yourself with others. In India & even in the world specifically, people have a lot of interest in your life, especially when you are in troubled times. To avoid the depression and isolation it is better to be in self-isolation & attend only constructive networking sessions &

seminars where people are with a razor-sharp focus on their agenda & nothing to do with your professional state. They would rather love to be in touch with people who are looking for alternative earning. It establishes many people in networking sessions, people with logical strategies; intentions to guide & train as this will add to their portfolio, induce collateral learning & collaborative earning. If you have no interest in a unique business, you earn a potential audience in the seminars by the exchange of numbers & cards. Learn to communicate.

No matter what people tell you, words & ideas can change the world.

-Robin Williams

SWOT Analysis

Now we have a situation in hand. No one can live on this earth without earning until & unless you have a rental income or other sources of income fetching you handsome amounts. Now, what should we do? Now is the time to know self with the use of management tools. The best tool for self-evaluation& is a very well-known tool used by various organizations for knowing their presence in the market & their threats & opportunities. The tool which is used to test the personality & skill set of the person is SWOT analysis. Albert Humphrey is the one who designed it; He was an American business consultant& coach. Albert designed this tool for a team output, the tools are very easy-to-use if practiced & used without a cheat. It is an important tool which will help you test yourself & know your key strengths, weaknesses, opportunities & threats.

The full form of the abbreviated tool is strengths, weakness, opportunities& threats. There are various videos, tutorials& presentations you can find online to make your own SWOT. To do a SWOT analysis, you will need a detail evaluation of your skills & gaps. This is not an individual activity as it may end up in complacency & it will have a negative outcome as either people find all negative in themselves or all wonderful pictures of self.

Involve a team of people i.e. friends, relatives, family members & even critics. These people together will help you make your right assessment as they know you well. They will help you as they also know this exercise is for your greater benefit. This activity will require sincere efforts & inputs.

They will contribute more on your weakness & your potential threats, which is a much beneficial input in the entire SWOT exercise. There will be many skills you only know about yourself but never tested it as a potential opportunity.

SWOT exercise requires an appreciable amount of introspection, as this exercise is a dynamic exercise which will require you to revisit & update. After this exercise, you will find improvements & changes. This will require updating your SWOT. It's a dynamic, detailed activity which can be updated from time to time after you work upon the opportunities, weaknesses & strength. After that, we have done the detailed exercise on SWOT analysis. It is time to work upon & reap benefits out of the exercise, to rise again with options in hand. I will detail a few of them which you can use & work upon the options best suited for you. Here we will work on strengths & opportunities only.

Key strengths identified:-

Public Speaking: -

This is the most, most, most important skill amongst all the professional, technical & personal skills. In every sphere of a professional life & personal life, the biggest fear in the life of a person is

a) Fear of public speaking & facing the public

b) Fear of death

If this one skill is there in you, you cannot fail under any of circumstances. The people with this art are the ones who can easily fit in any profile what so ever, as they can build a connection with customers with a lot of ease, colleagues, bosses & the subordinates. If you can communicate with an large set of audience with full confidence & with the specific content which people can relate to themselves; you can make any profession as your bread & butter; rather can have luxuries in life. You can connect with many potential customers using this art and combine it with the digital platform. You can share your learning's, train people, sell products, do Multi-level marketing, networking and set up an online business. One thing is sure, with this skill set you cannot fail in any sphere of life.

Technical: -

Your professional skills attained through your education &experience. It may be of IT, Manufacturing, Software, Chemistry, Technical write-ups. These are the skills are in demand which will never end; there will be a never-ending demand for these skills in the industry. You by your experience will be more comfortable with this. Explore how your technical experience can be of value by doing some seminars, write-ups, and blogs for these.

Operations: -

The experience of managing the working of the manufacturing setups and other operations like in KPO's, BPO's, Tele calling, Process industry, utility management, service, service providers & other such works. The capability to manage these operations can help you set up your venture. Operations are the backbone of the businesses; having all the departments working in sync to achieve a unified organizational goal is a big management skill. If you are good at coordinating interdepartmental activities & maintain a tempo to build upon consistent efforts to achieve a pre-defined goal as per strategy & budgeting is the core aim of operations. The key is getting all departments to synchronize.

Managing people: -

The master of all skills after public speaking is people management. The one's who know how to manage the headcounts & hand counts is the most successful of all. There is management saying "they do not expect you to know everything, but at least everyone knows something" If you are good at IPR (interpersonal skills), everyone knows at least something which is their USP. So you have multiple resources to accomplish anything in the world. This skill is the one skill which will never let you see a complete eraser of your existence as a professional. You will have many people, many brains, many hands & networks which will help you reinstate you & up-keep your employability.

Network Marketing & MLM: -

The buzz of the day is networking. Networking is using multiple levels of people connecting to achieve a bigger goal. Network marketing companies create small business owners with little or no investment. All you need to build is a chain or group of people who can align themselves to achieve their goals &dreams. People can earn at-least more than the possibility of a salary in their job. If you are consistent in your efforts & put in at-least 4 to 5 hrs a day every day, it is said that the chain created will have a never-ending flow of income. The investment of time, communication, learning, Intentions to grow, and at least 3 years of your life will have you achieve an income which can be much higher than a normal salaried & professional life. This field does not require too much of education. Even with a basic education but with sheer perseverance and consistent efforts, you can live the life of your dreams. There are many companies in India providing a workable platform, Training, skill sets& required details of products with the up-lines in the chain helping them down the lines to grow which add building blocks to their growth ladder. Some renowned MLM platforms are Forever Living products (FLP), Amway, Vestige, RCM, Herbalife, Oriflame, Tupperware, Modicare, Naswiz with ever-growing business & providing earning potential & opportunity for additional income to many of the people who are struggling to find the source of earning due to their lack of education, employability, communication, personality etc which are key requirements for getting used in Industry. The extensive free training provided by these companies is remarkable. You can bank on your social network skills to be successful in this field. **I have joined forever Living products & found them the best.**

Social & public events:-

This is also a way where you connect with many people. Social connections help you can find options to connect with people, opportunity & options which can give you a link to either organize events, Social gatherings, Laughter shows, marriages, corporate events, training & seminars, family day event in offices, outbound training, school trips etc. Managing marriages is like giving life to dreams of people. It is the biggest spend in the life of people in India. Marriages are more than just a social event & cultural requirement. It represents the status- quo. People spend most of their life savings in making these special moments of life memorable. Knowing their limitation to manage the event along with other social obligations people now outsource the marriage as it is a grand event, to highly professional companies giving potential employment to designer, flower decorators, catering people, Music band, dance teachers, designers & stylists, makeup artists, hosts, lighting, sound systems, fireworks, the list goes on & on. You can find the scope for yourself in the grand list with a million of these events taking place, especially in India with a young population in India with all religions having a similar passion & social status attached to marriages in the family.

Creativity: -

Being creative is a boon_you can create wonderful items, Projects school projects doing online assignments for schools, write research papers for PhD, help people doing multiple jobs do their unfinished tasks & aspirations. This will help you earn for yourself & family. There are 100 options if you have a special skill on creativity, just explore & search for options online to make use of it to the maximum. Creativity has endless potential; there is no limit to creativity. Being creative is just not limited to drawing & designing fresh things. It is a wide field involving creativity, a mind which can think out of the box. They require creative designers for designing sets, theme-parks, land-scalping, creating a space from a limited area, creative writing, writing poems, shayari, blogs & story writing. Writing songs, raps etc. Writing scripts for plays, movies, social messages, quotes, motivational messages can be a wonderful potential to earn.

Sales: -

Selling is a skill, which will never go waste, anything & everything in this world requires selling. If you are born with the special skill to sell; you will never be out of business. Starting from daily commodities to even the costliest equipment in the world requires selling. A minimum of 10~12% of the company's annual is budget allocated to sales & marketing. If nothing will sell, there will be no revenue. Selling is as important as the manufacturing of products & services to offer. The distribution and creating a sales network adds to the net worth of the business. The smallest commodities like camphor selling at 1 ~2 cents apiece also have a revenue model, which is not much known like other expensive commodities. In Asian countries like India, the daily business of smaller commodities may have a turnover of more than a 100 million INR. All it needs is a concentrated effort to connect with the right customer base.

Content-writing: -

Your creative skill with words is a brilliant way to express yourself, your thoughts or you may represent thoughts of others making it presentable. Content writing is in demand with many of companies & people outsourcing their content writing work to professionals with deep knowledge of the field & having the expertise in communication through words. You may or may not be a qualified person with a literature degree or a degree in journalism but if you are good at vocabulary & use of right words having originality & command on your topic. There is an enormous market & scope even with content writing companies & as a freelancer. Options are available for technical content writing, report writing, writing newsletters, promotional activities & literature for marketing companies, carry out press releases on behalf of corporate. All these require content writers. If you are a freelancer with credentials, you can earn a fortune.

Designing:-

Designing banners, Digital marketing content, Websites, furniture, Pamphlets, Textile designing, Fashion designing, Styling, Creating designs for brand promotions. You name anything which does not require designing, even food items like cake making, making food items displayed to look mouth-watering. It requires creativity, designing skills, hands-on with designing software. The automobile & manufacturing sectors are in continuous demand with people who are technically sound & are master in designing. "DC" is a well-known brand with an elite segment of people who get their vehicle redesigned to their taste. Furniture designing also has an enormous market with people planning to own a home want it to be their dream home with furniture being the inseparable part of it. The dream home requires dream furniture designed to be unique & is a very high-paying job. You can charge for your creativity. Interior designing is also one option where you design dream homes for people. People spend a maximum on three things in life, children's education, marriage & building dream homes. These provide a wonderful opportunity to earn.

Negotiation: -

The skill or an art, whatever we may define it to be. We require it in every role, even in managing homes. Managers needs to negotiate with the team; SCM people need to plan & negotiate deliveries and HR needs to negotiate while employing people, purchasers also need to negotiate to reduce the input costs adding to the bottom line of business. Now a day, global players in the business are hiring experts in negotiation to negotiate their business deals. You can use the expertise you have earned with your professional exposure to earn for yourself. Knowing your skill sets is always a great boon. Now a day's purchasing functions are being outsourced to the procurement companies who make deals on volumes & economize the buying thus passing on savings to end customers with a little /minimal % age requirements which make their buying more viable as compared to when companies do their buying themselves usually. These buying houses may be specific to the industry. Manufacturing sectors &

project-based companies hold e-biddings through these buying companies with professionals & hardcore negotiators on their board.

Product development: -

Many smaller manufacturing units cannot afford a high-cost team of people expert in their field of product-development. They outsource these jobs to the expert in product development who offers their service against a minimal professional fee. This is much more economical for the companies of small scale or companies which lack expertise in product development. These specialized companies are well aware of the vendor base, their capacity, their technical capabilities & know-how about the engineering products. Many companies have come up with set up for international purchasing based in low-cost countries like India, China, Vietnam, Philippines and Poland. This helps companies to reduce their cost of international travels & cost other management costs of business with having a professional set up in LCC reducing the cost of purchasing by using professionals, meeting their system requirements & procedures; working in alignment with their business goals.

Systems Consultants: -

Many organizations just survive in lack of systems.They need to have systems in place to grow businesses & to even become an international supplier. There is a requirement to meet the checklist of vendor evaluation for any business. Vendors need to qualify for ISO, IATF, OSHAS and many other internationally acceptable & recognized certification standards. The people with deep knowledge of systems can help small organizations to have systems & documentation in place. They can prepare a small business owner with technical potential & infrastructure to meet global requirement to benchmark the quality & documentation required as per customer. If you have certifications as an internal or external auditor from one of the various certifying bodies (having their base & international business exposure to their credit) besides the certificate you are having a relevant experience of the industry which gives you an added advantage. You can earn as per the number of days put in using your professional skill on having systems in place.

Data mining: -

Information is the key to the success of any business. Data is the feed for the marketing teams & consulting organizations. Now various companies earn in billions with their experts in data mining, data analysis & MIS creation. This information is the key input in many business houses which support & facilitate in their business decision making. Big data & Six Sigma are the key certifications along with certification of a project manager from PMI & PRINCE 2. Many ERP firms are working on creating these databases. SAP is one company in ERP which has created specific ERP modules generating MIS & reports to facilitate top management in business decisions. Companies like PWC, CRISIL & KPMG are the ones who are the front runners in generating reports related to specific businesses across the world detailing the trends, customer base, Voice of the customer which will help companies to re-design, robust marketing & sales strategy to target potential customer having need & the buying potential.

Auditing: -

Auditor is a person who carries out audits as their professional area of expertise. They conduct audits on behalf of various auditing bodies as system auditors and as financial auditors to audit financial books for various business organizations. It requires companies to submit their financially audited reports to theTaxation bodies of government, financial institutions & other interested parties. This is necessary from the taxation point of view; departments of government need to audit & need audited tax reports from the certified & credited auditing bodies & certified financial auditors. The financial books need auditing as compliance to keep & check to avoid any tax evasions and to ensure that all the companies, service providers, Professionals pay the due taxes to governments which is the source of revenue to run the financials of the country & to contribute to country's growth. Auditors with professional certifications, experiences & qualifications like CA, CFA, and Certifications as an auditor for manufacturing systems like ISO, IATF, OSHAS & other system compliances are in the key to business to comply with requirements of government & quality needs of the customer.

Financial Management: -

Not everyone is an expert in finances. The people who have grown in business starting from scratch with little or no knowledge of government compliances on VAT/GST returns, for labor compliances, Online reporting of returns related to taxes & even basic computation of taxes. The salaried employees also lack the knowledge to file their income tax returns. Here people having qualifications, experiences of liasoning with government bodies. This professional service is a symbiotic relationship between liasoning bodies, business people & the people involved in the management of financials. These people support the people in business & also the government bodies to ensure compliances and payment of the taxes & returns on time. It helps the collection of revenue as per due dates. The fees are nominal & most suitable for people with small businesses & part of MSME group. People get economical services at nominal fees & professionals get the volume of business. It is a win-win situation & also a wonderful opportunity for people who have required skills, experience & certification to carry out these functions.

Key opportunities Identified:-

Music

Singing

Painting

Interior decoration

Homemaking

Cooking

Video making

Data Analysis

Digital Marketing

Yogic arts

Astrology & Numerology

Physical Fitness & Diet

Candle Making

Counseling

Dress Designing

You can work upon these opportunities to convert them to your strengths. These are splendid opportunities with earning potential and they bring big satisfaction because you are doing what you love doing for yourself.

Think different & think out of the Box:-

The biggest challenge in the human world is that we always try to follow the set path only. We have defined study patterns, defined courses, selected & preferred professions. We strive to survive, struggle to perform, compete, create negative emotions for one another, do things which are not ethical, just in the competition to win the rat race, to be ahead by hook or crook. There is an endless struggle for existence whether you are in a job or a business. We are in continuous stress, pain, sleeplessness, negativity & challenging situation for our health. There is a very successful business community in India known as Marwari's who do off-track businesses, which usually appears to be tiny & does not invite any competition. When you study the business model & the profit, your eyes will ooze out in surprise. The amount they do is remarkable with profit margins ranging from 20~30%. The volumes go in millions. They specifically focus on businesses are out of the cut-throat completion technically coined as red ocean & focus on "Blue-Ocean "which does not have any fore-runners & the field is open for unlimited growth. The only focus is to increase volumes for the market. The demand is self-generated; it is purely on customer need basis. It requires a deep analysis of customer behavior, the voice of customer & demand gaps. Be ready with innovative, easy to use, and consumer-friendly solutions.

It is a surprising thing that these businesses run through generations without major changes just adding the volumes.They rather grow through ages with ever-growing needs & increase in demands adding to their pockets & profits.

The call of the time is to innovate & create some unique business idea, which works on the customer preferential products & demands. The vision is to explore the untapped market.

For Example: - There is a very strong trend of stand-up comedians, with people in their stressed up life need light moments. The Kapil Sharma show is an example where a light comedy & moments of laughter have made a celebrity & a millionaire out of a simple Amritsar guy. There was an enormous gap in this area & was untapped for ages. This is being filled by people like Amit Tandon, Jaspreet, and Nishant Tanwar to name a few and many others in standup comedy.

There is a market which has huge potential. This can generate revenue of over 2000 cr. Why focus only on traditional jobs, businesses & occupations, look beyond the routine, create, innovate & celebrate the new professional world.

Other options:-

Use your qualifications: -

 You can start tuitions for students who need support in studies. Parents now a day expect their children to perform the best to compete & be the front runners in their scores to clear competitive entrance examinations & even at school. People look for tutors for their kids after kinder garden & class 1st. We can use both group & individual home tuitions, which is also a suitable option with people who have carried out their education well. This is a fit revenue model & excellent work from home option.

Online data entry work: -

There are many options for online data entry work. Printing houses outsource data entry work. They base the pay perks on the number of pages. It can earn you up-to a few dollars.

Online earning:-

You can work for various sites & earn a suitable amount of money. There are many options available. Like Tee spring you can design clothing's accessories etc online & the creation, printing & distribution is taken care by the site. You will earn% age without investing, create, and promote your designed products online. There are YouTube videos to educate you. You can also become an Amazon business affiliate. You can promote Amazon listed products online &

Amazon will provide you a commission which is defined as per the product. Using internet & social media, you can earn a suitable amount of money.

<u>Pay per click:</u> - Many marketing companies look for online clicks & views for their clients & pay to people for adding several clicks. You can also earn by filling online reviews for companies. Pintrest is one of the companies where you also get paid for your creativity, online data & content creation where you also get paid as per their policy.

Option to work as guest professor or a Industry experts in colleges &universities:-

Many professional colleges & Universities across the globe look for experts & experienced professional from industry to give lectures & provide mentorship to the children who are eyeing a venture into their professional life. These experienced professionals are much sought after with their network, experience & exposure with industry. This can educate budding professionals about various functions in the industries, their work patterns, functionalities, departmentalization and correlations between departments. You can have an opportunity of starting with guest lecturers in universities & later on getting paid as you gain your grip. Universities offer the distance learning & also use freelance professionals for lectures for their part-time course students.

Online education: -

It is a very potent market as you can go a step ahead by creating your course contents & lectures with your practical experience amalgamated with your educational background which creates a natural edge for you to attract your online students. With the number of subscribers increasing over a few pre-decided numbers by YouTube & registering yourself with Google ad sense, you can have a revenue model with an increasing number of subscribers & views.

Similar to this, online video creation options like Tik-Tok, Hello & many other applications also add possibilities of revenues with the number of views increasing. There are many online options available for earning based on views & subscriptions.

Having assets which can an option of earnings like:-

Utilizing options of vacant rooms/Extra rooms for B&B: - There are many options available for B&B (Bed & Breakfast) options. Many travelers of the world look for hygienic & cheaper options to make their travel economical. You can explore the options with a brief formality with local authorities for approval.

Having a paying guest accommodation: - Students, Executives living away from their home town also look for safe & hygienic stay with home food. This is because their stay has to be long. You can offer rooms in your property with the option of 3 in1 room stay for an average size room & 5 in 1 stay options for bigger rooms with bunker beds. This can fetch you money to foot your bills.

Putting your property on lease with Service industries like OYO, ACCOR, BNB: - Companies like ACCOR, OYO have come up with the unique idea of stay for overnight travelers & day travelers. You can lease your property with 3 to 4 rooms to companies like OYO Rooms & can earn a handsome lease amount good enough to pay rents for smaller property & to meet your expense. These are options which you can explore in the time of crisis in job/earning.

Leasing out to corporate for ex-pats: - There are many companies having ex-pats on their management board. These companies look for an option for their accommodation which is fully furnished with full facilities & housekeeper to carryout daily chores. They pay a handsome lease amount for such properties. You can even offer the option of a premium vehicle with a driver. This could add on to your revenue & add value, reducing the on-cost of a loan for the vehicle.

Going ahead with renting of your property & moving in smaller but economical homes on rent:- You can plan moving out into a small & affordable rental accommodation & put your property on lease. This way the difference in rent earned & rent spent is a clear margin & saving.

Using Switch words & spirituality:-

Write the following Switch words to your use

Chant following:-–1176 DIVINE MAGIC BEGIN NOW

-GET-CHARM-COZY-COUNT-HAVEN-ON-

MAGIC–CARPET

-DIVINE ORDER BRING LETTER FOR JOB NOW

SOMEHOW WITH DIVINE SPEED LIGHT

-LOTUS-PARADISE-GET-COUNT-SURPRISE-

DIVINE

-DECLARE NICE CHARM GOOD NEWS WITH

SUBLIME COUNT

-FINALLY, BRING ENDORSEMENT CHARM

SUDDENLY SOMEHOW DIVINE

- WOLF MAGIC BEGIN NOW

-RESOLVE-ABIDE-RAINBOW-CHARM-ADD   COUNT–FINALLY-FLASH

-BRING RAINBOW CHARM GIVE TAKE 53 COUNT

-318514517618 write 28 times every day

-36343962 write 28 times every day

-741 write on the left hand with green color

-7135015 write 45 days 45 times

-520, 741, 808 write-on left hand to improve financial status

- 199621147 for monetary gains

Switch words are very renowned technique & known to work for almost 95% cases successfully. I find these to be very effective when the person practices these with full intentions. I have collected these from the switch word-groups, especially from Blue iris by Kat Miller & Divakar Manepalli. You can find these on their FB page.

https://www.facebook.com/groups/121402101824830/

https://www.facebook.com/KatThoughts/?__tn__=%2Cd%2CP-R&eid=ARDTqO3w3hlO6yrTESQekM7NqT_SFSX5-FJzgCwMV4xjX50ClP-ub681gwaVYzRrtemfoVASCgyfkAo4

Coming out of depression: -

We know Serotonin chemical to be a feel-good chemical. It is known that the lower level of the chemical in our body to cause depression besides physical & emotional state of mind.

To increase the level of this feel-good chemical does:-

Eat food like green vegetables, chia seeds, Cheese, beans & Kiwi.

Tea & coffee is also known as mood stimulators.

Exercise every day to release toxic elements.

Walk for at least 30 mines every day.

Sing.

Listen & dance on fast songs.

Chant universal sound "OM"

Listen to music & sound of flowing water.

Listen to the sound of Tibetan bowls.

Laugh.

Write.

Read books.

Listen to motivational videos.

Do self-talk.

Do a {What if exercise} the world does not end with a single failure. It is just a message that you need to re-look at the strategy you have used. One failure does not define your last destination. Life is much bigger than just a few unpleasant events. Getting up & getting going is a way of life. You may have to refresh everything & start from scratch. It is much better than going down without making efforts living with the situation. One stumble does not take away your ability to rise & start walking again. So chill! Re-look at your strategy, do the fine-tuning which is required & throttle back on track

A ready reckoner of Dos & Don'ts in the period of challenge:-

Do's

Keep your morale high as it is part of professional life.

Make a list of consultants with numbers & email ids.

Update your CV (restrict it to a two or max 3 page) & float.

Connect & call professional consultants to help find you a Job.

Connect with your mentors & professional references in the Industry.

Search Jobs through LinkedIn.

Identify your key skills & gaps.

Make a professional write up of your experiences as a case study.

Write every day.

Keep on learning through reading books, going through YouTube & Google.

Note down everything you come across.

Forward you're CV on Naukri.com & Other job portals on email id mentioned in the jobs displayed.

The chances of direct emails getting reviewed are much higher than the CV's sent through the apply button on Job portals.

Keep on updating your profile almost every week to exhibit your CV on people looking for a change in priority.

Take professional help with your CV making.

Write emails to follow up & call once in a week to check.

Be specific in jobs you are applying, check the match with your experience & expertise.

Search for your Plan B, like book writing, Blogs, training and network marketing, etc.

Call your previous employers to check for any job availability.

Respond to all calls, you never know which call is for you.

Keep your discussions short & crisp, both on personal & professional calls.

Check your email updates regularly to avoid missing any information regarding potential opportunities.

Reduce your financial liabilities like loans, etc.

Get a medical insurance for your family first.

Keep yourself fit, get into an exercise regime.

Spend time with your family

Don'ts

I did not find the use of taking paid resume circulation services through the job portal.

Do not make repeated calls to consultants as the desperation may degrade your professional value.

Avoid use of statements like "Desperately looking for a change." I advise not pay for resume registrations to consultants, Professional consultants do not charge from candidates.

Avoid not running from pillar to post asking for jobs.

I suggest not panicking & to stay organized & prioritize activities

Click any job on job portals after due consideration as there is a daily & monthly limit to jobs you can apply. Use it wisely.

Do not talk to gossip mongers. They are the ones who may leave look like an unpleasant event of your professional life.

Limit yourself &don't explain the reason for your exit to every Tom, Dick & Harry.

Do not speak badly about your previous organization during an interview on asking for your reason of leave.

Do not act like a sympathy seeker to get jobs, creating sad stories. Professionals look for winners in people & not the people with excuses.

Do not withdraw your PF & other retrials as these are for a longer future.

"You only are successful when you put your thoughts into action. Act now!"

Last but not least-

"Nothing is falling in your lap without effort, except the property & values you inherit from your parents,"

-Prabadip Ghai

About The Author

The Author of the book is Prabadip Ghai. Prabadip Ghai is a professional who is Industry expert, a competent Engineer, post-graduate in Quality management, PG Diploma in SCM & operations, Six Sigma BB and a Prince-2 accredited specialist. Prabadip Ghai is an accredited coach for six thinking hats, (parallel thinking De Bono), a poet, blog writer, a sacred healer, numerologist & a light worker. He carries over 25 years of Industry experience as a professional business improvement consultant & a corporate trainer. Prabadip Ghai is blessed with a wonderful life partner & two exceptionally smart kids name Rupahnshni & Prieyansh. Prabadip Ghai himself has been through sabbatical starting from scratch 3 times. He has tried his hands-on with many options stated in the book. He has worked with companies like JCB, Siemens, Faurecia and General Cable. The intention & effort to write this book is out of gratitude to universe & intent to help people through the challenging period which calls for a decision on profession & professional life. The aim & target is to reach a million people across the globe with a focus on helping more than a million souls. You can reach the author through various social media platforms stated below.

www. facebook.com/healingsoulnminds/

https://www.youtube.com/channel/UCI5S5GexSuXAT7m xdLm_1Lw

https://pradeepcghai.WordPress.com/

https://www.edbrains.in/

https://www.youtube.com/watch?v=KC55VZwnUWY

https://www.youtube.com/watch?v=6ukh7PiceCc

HOPE & EFFORTS ALONG WITH FAITH ARE THE BEST UNIVERSAL SUPPORT SYSTEM YOU HAVE

---PRABADIP GHAI